This is Your Life

Realizing the Power of Estate Planning and Asset Protection

Version 2.0

by
Michael D. Richmond

Warning

Before you buy an investment, insurance, or estate plan, always talk with a Certified Estate Planner™.

For a CEP® in your area visit the National Council of Certified Estate Planners website at www.nccep.cc or call 1-800-807-6988. the National Council of Certified estate Planners is an association of peers that monitors CEP's. It's purpose is to provide you with the best possible estate planners. Members in good standing have completed the CEP educational course and have shown themselves to be reputable.

The Liberty Institute 2000

Publisher: The Liberty Institute
Manager: Jason D. Richmond
Designer: Bill Moore and Jason D. Richmond
Printer: CPI

ISBN # 0-9656913-4-9

About the Author
Of This is Your Life

Michael D. Richmond
Executive Director of NCCEP

The founder of The Liberty Network is Michael D. Richmond. His estate planning roots go back to 1985 when he pioneered much of the marketing ideas for Revocable Living Trusts. Since then, he has personally taught over 2500 financial, accounting, and legal professionals in the basic and advanced ideas of estate planning. His belief is that estate planning is an art that allows a client to invest more wisely and keep their wealth secure. His credentials come more from field experience than formal education, which has made him a speaker and trainer in high demand.

·**B.Re.** -Bachelor in Religious Education
·**M.A.** - Master of Art in Administration
·**MCEP** - Master Certified Estate Planner
·**ISBA**- Illinois State Bar Association as a Paralegal
·Author of **"God's Money in Caesar's Pocket"** (co-author, Rex Black)
·Author of **"How to Retire in Seven Years"** and **"Judgment Proof and Tax Smart"**
·National trainer and editor of the **Certified Estate Planner** course
·Permanent member of the **National Council of Certified Estate Planners** (NCCEP)

Michael Richmond resides in the Chicago, Illinois area and has been married to his wife, Candy, for twenty-five years. They have three sons, two of which have followed him into business.

Contents

This is Your Life

Introduction

A new generation approaches their senior years. The for-ever-young group is now facing a new challenge. They are turning 50, and their outlook on life has once again created a market anomaly: the desire for estate planning. Their parents were more willing to trust in company pension plans, social security, and personal savings. However, the children are doubtful of the company's longevity, the government's ability, and inflation's long-term impact on their lives.

This generation has also watched their peers "crash and burn" as they were caught in corporate downsizing, divorce actions that destroyed families and wealth, business reversals, financial crunches, and civil litigation. We live in an age so proliferated by lawsuits that we have invented a new phrase: "Predatory Litigation" where personal wealth is gutted by incredible civil actions of greedy litigants. In other words, we may be looking at the most vulnerable and victimized population ever … and I doubt it will get better.

If you are a business owner, you face the most difficult of all the situations. You are the most exposed to lawsuits, the most taxed, and the most risk oriented of the American population. To the corporately employed, the idea of being a business owner appears far more rewarding than it actually is. Adding to these threats, the business owner faces an uncertain future if the business cannot be sold and provide the funds needed for secure retirement.

Three major concerns of the baby boom generation seem to be driving the marketplace to new heights. The employed of this generation fear these issues:

1) The concern in <u>job security</u>
2) The concern over <u>retirement security</u>
3) The potential of <u>total loss</u> of financial security

I am sure there are numerous other concerns, but they mostly boil down to one key element: SECURITY. In a volatile and unforgiving society, the boomers do not want to become the next victims. And they are far more demanding than any generation has ever been. But to their chagrin, they have turned to the financial gurus of their day and have once again been sold down the river through misguided advice.

You see, the age of mass marketing, narrow options, and governmental restrictions has turned the financial planners of this era into more sophisticated product peddlers. The boomers do not want to be treated as just "consumers," but one after another they are being sold varying versions of the same program. They all get into qualified retirement plans and invest their money into stocks, bonds, or mutual funds. We are being fed a sugar diet of product after product, but there is a dire need for comprehensive solutions instead of just making another investment. More and more, people are asking for something better than another minor patch on the problems of their life. People need a plan.

There are secrets to life, heath, and wealth that take time and money to discover. The trick is to get smarter before you get older and poorer. One of my goals in life is to help people attain the knowledge and access that the wealthy have enjoyed. The purpose of this book is to give you fundamental and critical insights that can make a huge difference on your life.

Do you realize that the IRS unfortunately sprang into existence in 1913? On the 1913 tax form, the imposition of a 1% tax was on those earning over $20,000. The tax of 2% for incomes over

$50,000, 3% for incomes over $50,000, and 4% for incomes over $100,000 is seen on the same 1913 form.

In 1999, if your income was $20,000, you are paying a tax of 15%. The income tax goes to 28%, 31%, 36%, and finally, the highest marginal rate of 39.6% if you are single person over $150,000 or a married couple over $250,000. Do you see a big change in the tax burden since 1913? This is why I say that we face a problem in these days called "Inflated Wealth." In other words, we are enduring "the problems of the wealthy without the resources of the wealthy."

In 1913, less than 1% of the American population earned $20,000 or more. This same people did not worry about capital gains tax, federal estate tax, as well as paying no income tax. Neither did he have to worry about an avalanche of lawsuits. My last point is that one million dollars was much more wealthy that the same million dollars in 1999. Today there are many, many more millionaires but the purchasing power of the 1999 millionaire has the reciprocal purchasing value of about $200,000 per the 1913 millionaire. We can't afford the advice of the truly wealthy!

Today, the average person must worry about money and the problems of money without the resources of the wealthy. We do not have the advice, resources, and tactics of the truly wealthy. Our growing economy has carried us into the realm of inflated wealth and we now endure all the problems of the wealthy. Consider the issues that we all face today that you cannot deny, but may suffer tremendous costs of tax, litigation, and other creditors.

I call them "Dangers to your Wealth." If we don't consider lawsuits, financial problems, and medical problems that may strike, consider that you may never have a problem, but you still face some very serious issues. All it takes is an adverse tax structure to turn your mountain of assets into a molehill. Taxes are a constant and oppressive adversary to your wealth. Taxes are not just a burdensome income tax, but the tax burden after tax burden that becomes oppressive. Consider the layers of taxes that we face over our lifetime:

Federal Income Tax	15-39.6%
State Income Tax	2-5%
Federal Estate Tax	37-55%
Gift Tax	18-55%
Capital Gain Tax	20% or 28%
Sales Tax	4-7%

We still must consider that a civil liability can strip away in virtual moments the wealth that took you a lifetime to develop. Divorce rates run between 52-57%, you have a one in ten chance of being sued, one-third of Americans either have had or currently have an IRS problem, and 1.4 million people (and climbing) go bankrupt every year. Over one million people go broke every year due to long term illness and apply to Medicaid. The FDIC runs on pennies versus the hundreds of dollars it insures. The national deficit goes unabated, and the certainty of tax rates climbing seems irrevocable. There are 20 million state and federal lawsuits filed every year. Attorneys earn over $30 billion in legal fees in civil lawsuit charges, and courts award over $300 billion in civil judgments each year.

So what good is a simple accumulation plan done by your investment person? Yet the typical financial planner who prepares your "Goals and Needs Analysis" only considers and proposes an accumulation plan and does nothing against the potential liabilities.

On the contrary, Americans are asking for, looking for, and finally, demanding PROTECTION or what I call ASSET PROTECTION. Will Rogers made a statement that applies powerfully today:

I am more concerned about the
.......RETURN OF MY MONEY
than I am about the RETURN ON MY MONEY

The advice about accumulation MUST be included in a plan to protect the client's accumulation. Therefore, there is a more pressing need for those who know how to grow your money to also include strategies to safeguard those assets from any unwelcome invasion.

If you stand in need of financial planning, I contend that you should not simply "Buy a Product" regardless of whether it comes from a <u>product provider</u> or the more sophisticated <u>financial planner</u>. The folly of "Buying a Product" in our society is almost too naive to be believed.

Instead, every family should first and foremost demand an estate plan that will address the other two key issues before you build the accumulation plan and purchase the products that are required. These two factors are:

#1- The Tax Impact of your future estate - Tax Plan

#2- The Civil Liabilities that you may face - Asset Protection

I strongly suggest that you should not purchase any investment product until you have done your estate planning. By an estate plan, I do not mean a Will and Joint Tenancy of your assets. Wills and Joint Tenancy can only be called an estate plan if you include the word "bad" in the phrase.

Does a concrete foundation make a suitable house? Does a set of tires and steering wheel make a car? Is a puddle of water an ocean? "No;" you should respond and say that these items are only part of the greater program. Well, as good as your attorney may be, he only supplies one part of a true estate plan … documents. Is your life insurance or annuities an estate plan? No; these are elements of planning, but they are not estate planning! Is your highly refined portfolio of stocks or bonds an estate plan? No; they are good but still just a shadow of what estate planning involves!

An estate plan is a "Roadmap" that will guide you to your desired destination by avoiding the pitfalls and providing directions until your journey's end. *This is Your Life* is your roadmap. A true Certified Estate Plannerä can create this plan and help you turn your financial journey into a certainty instead of a mystery.

In the brief pages of this booklet, I hope to convince you that it is time to make your foundation solid by preparing a plan that cannot be destroyed by adversity. And if you are able to accumulate a measure of wealth in your lifetime, no civil litigation, personal issue, or even economic tragedy can take away the security of your future.

This is Your Life is the only true estate planning program in America that will give you the benefits of security, accumulation, and tax reduction. I suggest you read each chapter carefully.

After all . . . This is Your Life

Whose money is it anyway? Throughout the material presented in this book, we will question the current advisors that you might be using. The intent is not to be caustic and denigrating, but to reveal that these advisors are simply ill-informed while licensed and hardworking. Those who feel obligated to their attorneys and accountants follow their advice to the point of blind obedience. The fear of IRS problems and civil litigation keeps them in power over many. The real question that should be asked is "Whose money is it, anyway?"

It is not your attorney's money, nor are we concerned that the attorney is able to buy his next Mercedes or send his children to an Ivy League college while you drive a Ford and struggle to put your kids through a community college.

It is not your accountant's money with his worries and concerns about taxation that seems to serve the IRS collection process more than your family. He is not as concerned about what you have left as he is worried about his billable hours and desire to steer clear of IRS questions.

It is your money that provides for your retirement and your comfort. It should pass to your children and the programs you support. It pays your bills, provides for your health, and purchases a portion of fun for the years of hard work.

It is your money! . . . . ***Isn't it?***

Chapter 1
How the Rich Do It

"Wealth is not an asset, it is a duty."

Have you wondered how wealthy people manage to hang on to their millions while you find it hard to live on the limited dollars you might save? We may resent this advantage, but the wealthy have had access to advisors who charge big dollars to develop planning that is far beyond what you and I receive.

Perhaps the most notable example is the two people who died within a year of each other. First, Jacqueline Kennedy Onassis died at age 67 with a gross estate valued at over $200 million. Parade Magazine told the story of how much tax she paid. Had it been you or I (with our simplistic planning), the federal estate tax (called death tax) would have been about $110 million!!! But her association with the Kennedy family and apparent sophisticated advisors allowed her to reduce her estate below the federal estate tax limits. This noteworthy accomplishment deserves a closer look!

How much did Jackie O. pay in death taxes? The answer is zero! She had so constructed her financial affairs that the federal estate was calculated at less than $500,000, which was below the

---

[1] As an interesting footnote, Jackie did slip up a bit and federal estate tax was applied. When several of the momentos were sold at Christy's auction house, they fetched far more than ever imagined. This did force her estate over the limit. We have yet to see what this amount was, but frankly it will hardly make a ripple in the vast wealth that was never taxed. Her son and daughter (and some charities) were the big winners.

$600,000 federal estate tax limit.[1]

The Kennedys have always had the finest estate planning device of any family in U.S. history, it seems. Starting with her marriage to John Kennedy, Jacqueline had made great use of the family's planning resources, and it has saved her family millions of dollars in taxes and legal entanglements.

Not many miles away (in Virginia) an attorney died with an estate of a mere $1.8 million. One of America's finest legal minds allowed his estate to fall prey to Virginia state and federal estate taxes even though he had personally designed a one-page will. Chief Justice Warren Burger delayed his estate planning until after the death of his wife.[2] He then sat down at a typewriter and typed up a one-page will conveying his total estate of $1.8 million to his son and daughter. The cost of his estate for these taxes was $450,000. That is nearly 25% of the estate lost by one of America's leading attorneys. He was the victim of his own industry's misinformation about wills! In that we credit the legal profession with such tremendous and omniscient wisdom, how can such a profound and intelligent attorney have suffered so badly? In this case, the typical advice of the legal community was ultimately a failure and disservice. The erosion of his estate by 25% should not be an example to follow, but a warning sign to those who value their life's financial accomplishments.

What was the difference? Jackie had a plan and Chief Justice Warren Burger didn't. Pure and simple, frankly stated, and clearly exampled.

Failure to plan is a plan for failure.

---

[2] On the day Mrs. Burger died, Chief Justice Warren Burger forever lost the ability to protect a second $600,000 of his and her estate through a simple A-B Revocable Living Trust. His use of a will thereafter reduced his exclusion to only $600,000 from the ravages of state estate and federal estate taxes.

You see, the wealthy demonstrate that they are wise as well as wealthy because they will seek advisors to provide them with above average advice. They don't seek advice from nominal attorneys, neither do they indiscriminately purchase investments, nor blindly accumulate wealth.

A person of sizable wealth brings together the best advisors to analyze his estate, and to consider his liabilities and tax concerns. The goal is to build an estate plan that will save him or her many times the cost of the plan. We call this assembly of advisors **The Rich Man's Table**, and it may be composed of these persons:

A true estate planning
Attorney
A Business Manager
A CPA or Accountant
An Insurance Consultant
An Investment Advisor
A Retirement Specialist
Other Trusted Advisors

In this first meeting, the clients disclose their financial information, personal wishes, and future concerns. It is now the job of this collective group to assemble a comprehensive estate plan that deals with the issues presented. Now, I don't know if you've ever tried to get a unified opinion from such a group of divergent professionals, but the meeting is a cacophony of ideas. It cannot be resolved in one day, one week, or one month. Months later, after numerous conferences, telephone discussions, memos, and faxes; your board of advisors completes your estate plan. None have been able to monopolize the project, but your plan is a compilation of ideas designed to address your needs and concerns.

It used to be that only the wealthy felt they needed such planning or were willing to pay for such assistance. Today, however, the constant inflation factor has forced us into large estate problems. An estate of $500,000 was a large estate thirty years ago, but now it is a modest estate. Today, a $500,000 estate is middle class and will likely grow into an estate of $650,000 in a few years. At that point, we now have the compounding problem of wealth ... generally considered taxation.

We make our estate plans in bits and pieces, and yet, our problems are complex. Life and death are no longer simplified; and yet we attempt to solve these problems with partial answers. We go to isolated advisors such as attorneys, accountants, investment advisors and have the naïve belief that their advice will solve a problem. Frankly, a will prepared by an attorney is not an estate plan.[3] Neither is a tax plan prepared by your CPA an estate plan. Even an investment by your insurance or investment broker is not an estate plan. We are not able to assimilate these divergent pieces of advice. So we must isolate ourselves to one or the other. By so doing, we seal our fate and fall prey to the problems that remain unaddressed.

DANGERS TO YOUR WEALTH

One reason we do not appreciate the importance of estate planning is that we are not aware of the stark array of problems that we face. Even the average person now faces large estate problems. There are numerous layers of taxes and fees that occur in and around illness and death. An example of these taxes and fees are:

Federal Estate Tax	37-55%
Probate fees	4-20%
Gift Tax	18-55%

---

[3] This is not an attack on attorneys or CPAs; it is a mere statement of fact. The multitude of issues facing the average or high net worth person are extensive and often

Capital Gain Tax	20%
Guardianship	2-4% of the estate
Medicaid	100%

The gross impact of these collective factors can strip 50-80% from an estate. It seems that few of us are aware of the pernicious factors that we face or how deep this knife will cut into our assets. A number of ancillary issues like "will contests" and family squabbles in probate court can run the fees even higher than expected. Even though your distribution plan is not complicated, the court and taxation system can make it a nightmare. Obviously, Medicaid can be the most devastating of all in the event of long term illness. Therefore, there is an immediate need for aggressive and competent estate planning.

PROBATE FEES AND DELAYS

The simple recommendation to prepare a set of wills and use joint tenancy seems to be the universal mantra promoted by most attorneys and repeated by those who absolutely trust their scholarly wisdom. In fact, as I hope to convincingly prove, this is likely to be the most absurd and  contrary advice possible. Without castigation, I believe that this persistent myth is propagated by the "Old Guard" as the "common fare" for the American public. Therefore, these advisors adopt the policy and pass it on to the less informed client. It is, nonetheless, at least dated, or at worst devastating advice. Yet, most people believe that they get quality advice from their advisors. But let's compare your financial situation to another similar situation. On the same day two men enter the hospital with similar ailments. One is very wealthy and the other can barely afford the day rate. Will there be a difference in their "quality of care?" Sure there will! And yet you believe that you are getting "quality advice" from your attorney or accountant. So, how much have you paid these people in the last five years for AD-VICE? The wealthy will pay $5,000 to $50,000 for these people to put the time into their tax, retirement or estate plan? Well, may I suggest that that is exactly the "Quality of Care" you are getting, and that is not good!

Probate is not cheap. The fact that most states have adopted simplified probate is almost irrelevant. To qualify for the simplified probate, your estate must be below the state limit. This limit is usually about $25,000 to $50,000. Now, how can anyone who owns a home and accumulates some measure of savings get below this incredible limit? The answer is to pass your assets to your remaining family members by joint tenancy. This is why the attorney will suggest a dual treatment of a will and joint tenancy. However, the second option can be even more devastating because it brings the likelihood of gift tax violations and capital gain tax problems. This advice may be legal, but it is absent of tax consideration. The fact that this advice will cause double taxation seems completely devoid of tax concepts, and yet it is a common suggestion to the blindly obedient masses.

Joint tenancy is suggested along with wills because any property that you hold in *Joint Tenancy with the Right of Survivorship* (JTWOS) will not be subject to probate.[4] So, the logic is that if you will hold nearly every asset you possess in joint tenancy with your heirs, your "probatable estate" will be below your state limits and you will enjoy the simplified probate process. What are the odds that this combination will happen? Well, someone just told me that a guy named Slim is packing a suitcase!

First, you will need to hold all real and personal property in joint tenancy with your spouse and subsequently with your children.

---

[4] It should be noted that JTWOS does provide an interim solution at the first death. Since we have unlimited gifting with a spouse, we will not have a gift tax at that point. Our reference of adverse effects are primarily pointed toward the second death and putting other persons on title that are not a spouse.

An examination of the issues in such actions reveals the following problems:

1. The surviving spouse will have capital gain tax on half the gain realized at the sale of an asset causing unnecessary taxation. (Other than family residence)

2. Civil liabilities of other joint owners may bring recovery action against your property. This means that children on titles or accounts with you increase your liabilities.

3. Loss of control by the parents if the children do not agree with your disposition of assets. Remember that they are legal signers now on the accounts, and you may not borrow or sell property without their approval and signature.

4. The day you give a non-spouse any real or personal property over $10,000 per year, you cause a gift tax that can be compounded by penalties and fines if not paid in the same year that the gift was actually made. IRR 25.2511(h)

5. The surviving joint owner will be hit by capital gain tax on their portion of the capital gain on the day of sale even after your death, since JTWOS receives only a ½ step-up at death.

6. IRS will impose the Federal Estate Tax on the first person to die. In this situation, it is possible to have a child precede you in death and trigger federal estate tax on the assets you put in joint tenancy with them.

The latent problems of joint tenancy are so imposing and persistent that it seems no advisor would suggest it without grave warnings of the consequences. Another problem is that, over the years, the senior will not keep everything in the name of the children since there is a desire to maintain a level of privacy and a measure of uninterrupted personal control. Therefore, the natural tendency will be that few estates will ever go through simplified probate, and the compounded problems of joint tenancy will only exacerbate the problems.

FEDERAL ESTATE TAX

Perhaps the largest tax that you will ever pay is federal estate tax (also called "death tax"). America is one of the few countries in the world that charges a death tax, and this fact has kept American families from passing wealth from generation to generation (like Europe). Europeans understand such ideas as "Old Money," meaning that once a family reaches a measure of wealth, it stays for generations because it is not adversely taxed. The job of the younger generation is to preserve the family wealth. Federal Estate Tax is one of the main reasons your wealth may not reach the next generation, and almost certainly will not reach your grandchildren.

Currently, Congress imposes a 37-55% tax on any part of your estate that goes over $675,000.[5] The Taxpayer Relief Act of 1997 allowed for a gradual increase in the exclusion amount by raising the $600,000 by $25,000 per year until it reaches an ultimate level of one million dollars. Now, this probably sounds like good news, doesn't it? Well, it is! However, let's consider this in light of the potential increase in estate values. You will discover that the latest tax concession is similar to a Band-Aid on a gushing wound. It is certainly a measure of relief, but does not truly address what is happening in the real world of finance. Over the last ten years of the financial markets, we have historically experienced far more than a 4% annual growth in real estate and financial products.

The numbers game of Congress continues to confuse the true issues of economic impact. Below, is a chart of the current 1997 $600,000 allowance followed by the new federal estate tax which increases over the next ten years to demonstrate the point. Depending on your investments and success in asset growth, you can now see

---

[5] You actually have a $211,300 unified credit that offsets the federal estate tax of $211,300 on the first $675,000 (as of 2000). The rate of 37% is that level of the graduated scale that applies once the credit is exhausted. The effect is that you are taxed for amounts above $675,000 (or higher).

what the current federal estate tax allowances might mean in real life. If your growth exceeds the 12% range, the impact is even greater than we've illustrated, and the need for more intensive planning is evident.

You might note that it allows only a 4% maximum growth on your estate. Then consider an 8% and 12% return using the same $600,000 starting point:

	FET	Growth	8% Growth	12% Growth
1997	$ 600,000	0%	$ 600,000	$ 600,000
1998	$ 625,000	4%	$ 648,000	$ 672,000
1999	$ 650,000	4%	$ 699,840	$ 752,640
2000	$ 675,000	4%	$ 755,827	$ 842,957
2001	$ 675,000	0%	$ 816,293	$ 944,112
2002	$ 700,000	4%	$ 881,597	$1,057,405
2003	$ 700,000	0%	$ 952,125	$1,184,294
2004	$ 850,000	18%	$1,028,295	$1,326,409
2005	$ 950,000	11%	$1,110,558	$1,485,578
2006	$ 1,000,000	5%	$1,199,403	$1,663,847

There is real concern on the part of the author that the TRA of 1997 is too heavily weighted on the latter end of the scale, and that no tax bill will endure eight to ten years. The TRA of 97 is the first tax reduction bill in sixteen years. The last tax reduction bill was in 1981, and suffered very badly from a series of subsequent tax bills that removed most of the virtues and stuck us with larger taxes in order to "balance the budget."

The euphoria of the new tax cuts to the average taxpayer will lose support as we approach the year 2002, and discover we are not going to reach a balanced budget. The facts are clear that Congress and the White House have balanced the budget on the expectation that we will continue to enjoy a growing economy (shades of Reaganomics). This is all predicated on the current robust economy of 1993-1997. In fact, many feel the sixteen-year increase of the economy reaches back to the Reagan tax cuts and business incentives. Regardless of the credit or blame, it seems less than reasonable to believe that we will enjoy an uninterrupted economic boom without some periods of downturn. So, the expectations that we will grow our way into a balanced budget by 2002 is a fool's errand but plays well to the public. For this reason, I am dubious of the $1,000,000 federal estate tax allowance in 2007.

What will happen if the economy does steam roll ahead? What if they discover that the national debt is increasing, that Congress cannot trim spending, and the economy does grow at the current extraordinary rate? The answer is very clear. We are more than likely to see the repeal of tax incentives and the imposition of similar pre-1997 tax rates.

Finally, do you realize what will happen to $600,000 that was not subject to the Federal Estate Tax in 1997, but grows at a 7% annual return? The account will grow to $1,200,000 by simple compounding, which is $200,000 over the $1,000,000 limit. By doing nothing by getting a nominal return, you will have a Federal Estate Tax problem. By the way, you tax bracket has also krept up to 41% making your "Death Tax" about $81,000. Planning pays!

DANGER: TAXABLE RETIREMENT PLANS

It should not be forgotten that all these plans will still be subject to income tax when you withdraw your money (except the Roth IRA).[6] The concern that tax rates will rise above the current 36% ought to be calculated. With Canada at a 53% tax rate, Germany at 49%; it is not unreasonable that you may draw your retirement money out at an unfavorable tax rate.

---

[6] The Roth IRA (named after Senator William Roth) allows non-deductible premiums but tax free distributions regardless of whether the money is drawn from principal or interest. This is new with TRA 1997.

I am further concerned about a fickle Congress and their constant changing of qualified retirement plans. The Roth IRA is a great idea, but I feel like there's another shoe that hasn't dropped yet. The ability to have a tax advantage doesn't seem to stick around for very long.

Under IRC 1980(c) any portion of your retirement plan that passes to your heirs will be included in your federal estate tax. As you may now understand, taxation takes a huge toll on your wealth leaving much smaller than expected amounts to your loved ones. This also creates a "Double Tax Problem" since the qualified plan may also trigger Federal Estate Tax as well as the required Income Tax.

DANGER: LIVING PROBATE OR GUARDIANSHIP

It has been said that Probate will be a $294 billion industry in the next decade.[7] The eager attorney world is more than happy about this prediction. After civil lawsuits, probate and transfer of estates is the second largest source of attorney income. The national average of 7% is the likely toll on most Americans, but the fees to probate an estate can range from 4% to 20% or more. Norman Dacey pointed out that "Probate is a voluntary tax levied by the legal profession upon the rest of the population."[8] His remarks were not incorrect, and in fact they were painfully true! The average public is duped into believing that wills and joint tenancy are the best recommendation for the unwashed masses. This is obvious conflict of interest! This advice is followed as gospel by the average family. In that the attorney gets control of the "Living Probate" during disability and the estate at death, he is always well compensated for advising clients to use wills. In

---

[7] The Millionaire Next Door, Thomas J. Stanley and William D. Danko, Longstreet Press 1997. This is an excellent book that looks into the very real future for a visit of financial realities that your children and grandchildren will face.

[8] How to Avoid Probate, Norman Dacey. Dacey could be called the father of the Living Trust movement. While it is a book that lawyers refute, it is a great book.

fact, everyone who writes about the failure of the probate system will be criticized profusely by attorneys.

Living probate occurs when the client does not die, but becomes unable to conduct his affairs. Even the spouse is rendered helpless by the courts though he or she is otherwise totally capable of handling the financial affairs. Living probate is also called guardianship or conservatorship. Regardless of the name, the impact is humiliation and endless legal and accounting costs. It also takes the ability to control your affairs from you and your spouse and places it with the courts. Not a good trade!

In such cases, your estate will be subject to court control and continued fees during such period of incapacitation, and you are left without the ability to decide your financial future. In Fairfax County, Virginia, a judge reported that she had over 400 active conservatorship cases. It is more than safe to say that when each state and county cumulatively estimates the number of guardianships represented, there is several billions trapped by the courts and conservatorships throughout America.

The **Dangers to your Wealth** compound and begin to destroy the years of saving and investing for which you have sacrificed and labored.

MOST PLANS ARE UNPLANNED

Regardless of your investing or work retirement plan, few people have considered all the potential problems we face in this modern society. We need to list the numerous issues that go unplanned in the lives of most families:

Income Needs: To assure your financial stability

Medicaid Planning: To provide senior illness protection

Capital Gains Tax: Loss of 20-28% of all profits in federal tax

Marital Problems: 57% national divorce rate

Lawsuit Protection: To become judgment proof

Qualified Money: Taxable at uncertain future tax rates

Investment Needs: Structure of investments to your needs

Income Tax Help: Employ strategies to reduce taxes

Business Planning: Planning that keeps your business alive and in the hands of people you choose

Charitable Giving: Assure your social income matches the things you believe in.

Wealth Development: Strategic formation of a plan that assures your wealth will not erode in one generation.

If I were to paint a picture of most families' estate plan, I would list all these issues in an unorganized array and place a huge question mark in the center of the page. The mere fact that you have one or more investment, insurance, or retirement plan does not mean you have ordered your affairs. A true esate is far more than several investments, but a game plan to protect your portion of wealth.

We are told that a person spends more time planning a vacation than their retirement or estate plan. Immediacy plays a factor in this since vacations are more fun and often a few months away. In the long view of our lives and life expectancy of this generation, making sure you have your affairs in order is very important. Assuring that your children and grandchildren will enjoy a portion of your estate actually extends the value of your estate planning.

When told by the judge that he would be going to jail for a long time and that he should get his affairs in order, the man replied, "Judge, now that I'm going to jail, the only order I can put to my life is to shoot my dog, burn my house, and tell Nellie to not quit her night job."

We are told that there is one thing for certain, and that is that nothing is certain. If it weren't for accidents, they could close most hospital emergency rooms and stop putting bumpers on cars. A serious estate plan must look at the stark realities and potential problems and find solutions before the problems arrive and not depend on government redemption. Accumulation is not king, and the need to resolve tax concerns and civil liabilities adds extraordinary value to your planning. Without a plan, you are vulnerable and an easy target for the problems of life. You fall prey to the costly and pathetically slow processes of the State and legal system. You fail to complete the process that took you a lifetime to establish. It seems an impossible concept that we fall short of protecting our wealth.

Chapter 2
Estate Preservation

"COD - The Cost of Dying and Disability"

Estate Preservation means that you wish to have your assets pass to your heirs with little or no erosion. The factors against a successful transfer of wealth to the next generation are difficult or at least problematic. The transfer of wealth by the current generation exposes over $11 trillion to factors that are adverse to your plans and your family's needs.

PROBATE - WHEN THE COURT TAKES OVER

Do you think a will is an effective transfer device for your weath? Well, it isn't! Whether you have a will or not, if your estate is over $25,000 to $50,000, your estate will go through Probate. And frankly, probate is an adverse process if you wish to provide effectively for your family members.

Regardless of whether you think that probate runs 4%, 10%, or 20% it is still a completely unnecessary cost factor. Attorneys argue that Probate is not expensive and serves a meaningful purpose in transferring your estate. If your estate is over the simplified levels, your assets will be subject to the delays and costs of probate court.

---

[9] Probate: AARP "Consumer Concerns and Perspectives" (1990) was a two-year study on probate. An article written by Attorney Armond Budish concluded that "Probate is costly, slow, and outmoded . . . a sad state of affairs." The complete article can be found in Modern Maturity magazine Aug/Sept 1991 issue.

Such delays can take one to two years and will cost an average of 7-10%. AARP has researched the subject of probate more than any other source.[9] Without exception, every non-attorney source generally agreed that probate is a bad idea and a poor estate transfer device.

Since there are three (and only three) ways to transfer your assets at death, which one is better? The three options are:

1) Wills that are processed through Probate
2) Joint Tenancy with right of Survivorship
3) Contracts such as Trusts and Insurance

Device	Delays	Costs	Step-Up in Basis
Wills	1-2 yrs	7-10%	Full Step Up
JTWROS	None	None	½ Step Up
Trusts	None	None	Full Step Up

Let's suppose you go to a fine attorney to have a set of wills prepared. It takes $500, several months, and three meetings to accomplish the task. As you leave the attorney's office, you are pleased with the thought that you have completed your estate plan and your affairs are in order.

Now here's the real question. Is your attorney-prepared will binding upon the probate judge at your death? The answer is "No!" Some have called a typical will nothing more than a "Letter of Wishes." Your will is an expression of your wishes, but does not have binding control over the judge. In fact, while the judge will generally follow

---

[10] A will contest is when one of your family members or heirs contest the will and ask the judge to provide relief by altering the will structure. This often precipitates a family feud as one sibling struggles with the other siblings. The result is families who become totally alienated by hate.

your wishes, he may also set aside or alter your will!

We are told that one-third of all will contests are successful in altering or overturning the will. [10] Now remember, you paid a fully licensed attorney to prepare these legal documents, but they are not legally binding on the probate judge. In fact, the judge has the power to set aside your will and impose his own estate plan if he deems it necessary! How does this make you feel about wills now?

Another matter of concern is that probate is calculated on your gross estate, not your net. Regardless of your mortgage, credit card balance, or car loan, your probated estate does not include debt … only assets. You may own a $100,000 home but you have a $90,000 debt. Your real estate alone will go through full probate, and they will probate $100,000 (not your $10,000 in equity). This is true for all manner of assets and your net worth statement means nothing; it is your gross worth that they calculate. You will find that life insurance is not included in the probate estate when correctly installed.

DISABILITY: WHEN THE COURT TAKES OVER EVEN EARLIER

Do you think your spouse can run everything after you become ill? By all sound thinking, they should have the ability to run the family affairs, but this is not so in America. Without special care, the spouse is not allowed to handle jointly owned assets without court approval. This is known as "Court Appointed Guardianship," and it is definitely something to avoid.

If you follow the advice of the attorney and have a set of wills prepared, then you have agreed to hold everything in joint tenancy. You should consider what it will take to dispose of assets when one spouse is incompetent. In fact, no spouse has the automatic right to sign the name of the other spouse regardless if they are well or sick. Literally, you are disenfranchised by your faulty estate plan, and may be forced under court supervision of your own assets!

Suppose Mom needs to cash some stock or sell a piece of real estate to provide for extra money for the family. She goes to the stockbroker and directs him to sell the stock. He agrees if she and her husband will sign the necessary forms. She informs him that her husband is ill, and she will simply sign the forms for him. Any proper broker will tell her that is illegal, and she needs to see an attorney who will help her get court-appointed guardianship over her husband, whereby she can then sign the forms for the sale of the stock.

Mom now learns that she doesn't have a free hand, but must pay all the fees for the proceedings. She will have to report every penny she receives and spends to the court annually. From that day forward the courts and attorneys will rule over her and the assets of the family, and that she does not have freedom to run her affairs.

The spouse cannot sell the car, borrow money, cash in a mutual fund, stock, bond or annuity without both signatures. In theory, she cannot cash the retirement or pension check at the bank either. (An uninformed bank may let such issues go unchallenged). The impact of a major illness or stroke may leave the spouse totally unprepared and helpless. So, she is sent to see her attorney.

The answer to this problem is exceedingly simple, you must have either a Power of Attorney for each spouse or you need to have your assets in a trust where either may act as trustee or manager under trust authority. In such cases, the court's job is done and the well spouse can effectively carry on the family affairs.

Courts have literally tens of thousands of estates and millions of dollars tied up in their painful oversight. Such a fact only reveals the huge deficit in proper planning by countless families and the result is far more punitive than might be imagined by the non-attorney world.

Chapter 3
Predatory Litigation
"Sharing your Wealth with the Plaintiff"

IT FELT LIKE A HEART ATTACK when the sheriff handed Jack a summons from a person who he never thought would do such an incredible thing. Jack nervously read the numerous accusations until he reeled at the amount they were seeking. $800,000!!! How in the world could anyone believe that a small episode could be worth that much money? He called his attorney and got the first appointment he could arrange. After reading it over, the attorney said he could defend him, but not until Jack put up a $4,000 retainer. That might not be enough to cover all costs if they go to court, or if other problems arise. Jack explained to him that this suit was ridiculous and that he was not at fault. The attorney's response was "that didn't matter," but (like it or not) Jack's fate was in the hands of a judge whom he'd never met and his attorney, who until recently only handled his traffic tickets and also specialized in divorces and bankruptcies.

The next two years of Jack's life were a mixture of agony, worry, and uncertainty. Periods of anger and protest made no difference in the non-personal filings, motions, and pleadings. The attorney encouraged Jack to settle with the plaintiff for $100,000 plus attorney fees. Jack was so mad that he wanted to grasp the collective court by the neck until it realized he was innocent. In fact, he now felt like the victim. But the attorney said if they went to court, the judge could award them even more. Jack's life was a nightmare. His wife worried too. There were moments when he saw doubt in her eyes, and there were spells when he could barely keep his mind on business. Wasn't there something they could have done? According to his attorney, that was just the way the system worked. To that, Jack said, "Well, then the system stinks!"

Had there been a chance to go backward in time, there was something that could have been done. It is called asset protection. Jack didn't realize it, but there are two phases to proper estate planning, had there been the opportunity:

Estate Preservation: Which means that we endeavor to pass your estate to your heirs with minimal delay and cost. This is the first level of estate planning which prevents erosion of your family assets by unnecessary court proceedings and taxes.

Asset Protection: Which means we try to protect your assets during your lifetime from loss. This is the second level of estate planning whereby we are forced to provide a legal protection of our assets that attorneys or courts cannot promise. Asset protection is a legal fortress erected prior to a legal attack. The result is greater security.

Both Estate Preservation and Asset Protection should be accomplished a long time before such problems ever come up. Most people just wait too long, believing that the statutory system of state, civil, and probate courts are their only and best defense. Your estate plan could be a better defense than your attorney!

Representative Radkin from Minnesota has stated that there are twenty million lawsuits filed every year in state and federal courts of America. You have a one in ten chance of being sued, and there are 800,000 attorneys who are under-employed and under-paid. We have even invented a new term for American attitudes toward lawsuits: **"Predatory Litigation and Professional Plaintiffs."** It is hard to believe, but there are many people hoping to find any cause to sue someone with deep pockets. And worse yet, they predict one million attorneys and 40 million lawsuits in the year 2000.

The vast majority of greed-motivated people may never win at the lottery, but they may win handsomely in court. Sure their attorney will take one-third in settlement, but a settlement or judgment is a windfall of money. They will be hoping for any size settlement that will pay off a few bills and afford them a nice vacation while you are left to sort out your life in the aftermath.

We pay attorneys $30 billion per year for legal service during lawsuits and the courts award $300 billion in awards! Where does that $30 billion in legal fees and $300 billion in court awards come from? If you just felt for your wallet in a moment of ill-at-ease, you already know the answer.

Innocence is no Defense! Regardless of what you may feel is fair, the judge and opposing attorneys may not agree. The concept of liability is built upon two precepts that most non-attorneys do not appreciate:

Liability Forming Action: This means that you did something that caused an injury. Motive is irrelevant until they decide on the size of the award. Therefore, it does not matter to the court that it was an accident, that there was no malice, and you never anticipated potential harm. If you throw a stone at a dog but hit the neighbor's child, the judge will look beyond your motive to the fact that you intentionally threw a stone.

Proximate Cause: Were you the one who was closest to the damaging action? We'd all like to blame someone else for the problem, but you were the one who was most closely associated to the injury. In a breach of contract where you fail to deliver a product, will a judge dismiss the case because your workers were on strike? Will an auto injury claim be deterred because you thought you had the right of way? In both cases, you are the person that will be liable for damages.

Certainly our society is trained to put confidence in their attorneys to protect their rights in such improper legal actions. However, consider that your attorney cannot guarantee a victory in any court case. He may believe he will win, but ask him if he's ever lost a case that he thought he should have won? And also ask him, "If we lose this case, can we limit the damages the judge awards?"

The problem is that we rely upon attorneys to protect us instead of ourselves. Every person needs to carry insurance to protect the injured parties of accidents, but they also should create an asset protection plan within their estate plan to protect themselves. With increasing popularity, the use of trusts, limited partnerships, and limited liability companies are the devices that are being demanded for such matters as estate preservation and asset protection.

In the chart below, we show the two areas of civil protection: The Courtroom, where we depend upon the attorney; and your estate plan, where you depend upon a personal defense.

Courtroom	You	Your Estate Plan
Your Attorney		An inheritance plan
Lose the case =➔	Your Assets	Safe Haven

As you can see above, if your attorney loses the battle (in part or whole), what can the plaintiff reach? The painful answer is you and all that you own. The typical estate plan does only one thing. It will pass what is left of your estate to your heirs. In many cases this is enough, but as civil litigation and ownership problems grow, you need protection today. We advocate that asset protection will change the way you own your assets by placing them into your estate plan where civil courts cannot reach.

Courtroom	You	Your Estate Plan
Your Attorney	Few Assets	Your Real Wealth

In this simple example you can see a vast difference. If you move ownership out of your name and into the name of your estate plan, your creditors may win in court but be unable to strip away your assets because of change of ownership prior to the liability.[11]

In many ways, attorneys and accountants rule us since they dictate the terms of our lives. Such issues, as liability-forming action, are the occupation of attorneys. Therefore, we spend our time avoiding potential problems rather than in the pursuit of business. It also makes life extremely complicated and noisome. Yet, there seems no relief in sight except to buy more and more malpractice insurance.

A plumber in Indiana attended a seminar that I conducted about advanced estate planning and announced that he had been sued three times. He explained further that he had successfully defended each case and walked away a winner. But his third statement shocked the audience more than I could have ever done. He said, "The fact is that it has cost me nearly $20,000 to defend myself each time. Mr. Richmond, I can't afford to win any more lawsuits!"

America is the land of the eternal lawsuit. We may ignore the obvious threat of our day before a judge because we feel we have no answers. I remain adamant about the statement that your estate plan needs to have asset protection as part of the 21st century requirements.

---

[11] Trusts are the most effective device in these instances. They allow you to partially or completely remove ownership from yourself. Holding title in a trust is a simple process but very misunderstood by the general public and unfortunately by the legal profession. The most effective way to hold title away from creditors is in a fee simple method, where legal and equitable title is held in the trust name and you retain only contractual beneficial enjoyment.

If you are a business owner, I have more bad news. Of the one in ten people that can expect a lawsuit, you are ten times more likely to be sued if you are a businessperson. If you are a hard working businessperson you are 25% more likely to suffer a divorce. You are also 36% more likely to retire with less than sufficient funds due to the many issues you face. You will work harder and some attorney is waiting for his phone to ring and start the clock on billable hours. Makes you wonder why they even try, doesn't it?

RESISTANCE TO TORT REFORM

The legal system has had a total resistance to tort reform. In case you are not familiar with torts, the word tort refers to injury, damage, or loss suffered by another. Since this is a civil matter, we might relax for a moment knowing that you won't end up in jail. [12] However, the emotional, marital and financial stress you suffer might make six months in jail seem easier. Civil litigation can last three to four years, cost more money than you might imagine, and offers no assurance that you will walk away unscathed.

Innocence is no defense in such matters regardless of how sincerely you feel you were right. The court reserves the final judgment, and you will have very little to do with the proceedings. The process seems to run outside your control as depositions, petitions, motions, and pre-trial hearings disenfranchise you from contributing.

I'd like to tell you that getting a good attorney will force a

---

[12] There are two basic courts for settling wrongdoing. The criminal courts deal with criminal wrongs such as misdemeanors or felonies and you can go to jail if found guilty. The civil courts deal with matters of equity or fairness where the rights of another have been damaged. You will not go to jail for civil liabilities, but your wallet will suffer great damage.

positive conclusion to the matter, but it won't! Regardless of the price, skill, and experience of the attorney, he cannot guarantee a win in the court. A good attorney is an asset but not the decisive factor in a court battle. Ultimately, you will endure years of uncertainty, spasms of anger, and periods of melancholy as the wheels of justice grind slowly along. We're just not certain who will get ground-up in those wheels, however.

Finally, the last insult. Several years later (and many dollars poorer), we arrive at the day of decision when the court will finally decide the case. The feeling is incredibly disconcerting as you find that the next few moments holds your financial fate in the balance. If the decision goes against you (as incredible as it may seem), you may lose a very large portion of your personal wealth. This is truly insult upon injury.

In summary, I want to make a profound point. Do not trust courts nor place your total faith in attorneys. Build your estate plan in such a fashion that it includes asset protection or judgment proofing. If your attorney fails or the court makes that incredible decision against you, you will thank the day that you structured your plan to safeguard your assets from civil creditors. If you place your total confidence in the American system of jurisprudence, you are in for a devastating wake up call.

As divorce rates climb, businesses struggle, bankruptcies increase, and lawsuits abound, the smartest thing you might ever do is to put a legal distance between you and direct ownership of your assets. In so doing, you may rejoice when others would cry, and you may survive when others wish for death.

I want to make one final note that you may or may not appreciate, but the picture is far too vivid to pass by without comment. O.J. Simpson fought both a criminal and civil case in the courts as millions watched. First, he was acquitted of the criminal charges with certain credit to the "Dream Team" of attorneys that he assembled.

This was without doubt an amazing event of court history, and a lesson in asset protection for all of us.

Secondly, O.J. was brought into civil court over the deaths of Ron Brown and Nicole Simpson. Again he was well defended by attorneys, but this time he was held liable for their injury and death. The first award was for $8.5 million for civil damages. The second award for punitive damages was $25 million. Now let me ask you what O.J. was doing the very day (if not the hour) that the jury awarded the $25 million to the Brown and Goldman family? He was playing golf. Had that been you or I, we would have been in church praying or in the courtroom sweating.

We were later told by Peter Jennings and Nightline that O.J. Simpson had set up several irrevocable trusts for the benefit of his children that would not be subject to the court's reach. It is reported that he had F. Lee Bailey purchase property for him in Florida (which has homestead laws that civil courts cannot reach), and his trip to Oxford included a substantial movement of cash to non-U.S. jurisdictions. O.J. Simpson has worked as hard on defending his money as he did on his legal defense.

Regardless of what you may think of O.J. Simpson, he has amply demonstrated the vast importance of having a plan for your assets in case of any unexpected and devastating events. He does demonstrate in poignant fashion the need for a plan to protect and preserve your assets. Few will come close to the calamities of O.J., but the impact of a lawsuit is no less traumatizing. And the ability to withstand and even survive intact through such legal actions is a tremendous advantage.

Chapter 4
Taxation and Inflation

"Money That you Cannot Keep"

Perhaps the two fundamental reasons that American families cannot amass wealth and pass that same wealth to the next generation are taxation and inflation. In fact, 80% of current millionaires did not inherit their wealth. Unlike Europe, where wealth spans multiple generations, American wealth does not pass to more than one or two generations. While almost every country taxes its citizens, few countries impose a death tax similar to America.

Taxation is more insidious than most realize. The power of taxation is not only the power of income tax, but also a series of taxes that can compound into a punitive and confiscatory burden to every American family. The progressive tax system means that the more you make, the more they take. Adding to the progressive tax, we have other taxes that fall on the wealthy, (federal estate tax, capital gain tax, and excise tax) and you can easily see why wealth is being stripped out of every generation in America. This creates a dire necessity for each generation to struggle against the odds to achieve a measure of security. It seems that the largest heir to most estates is the federal government who will doubtlessly spend your inheritance in a fashion that will bring you and your children delight. Actually, such endowments to the government are a contribution to bigger and more intrusive government policies. The more you feed the government, the more aggressive it becomes.

Incredible as it may seem, taxes have never been reduced in anything other than token and short-term movements. The trend of taxation has always been ever increasing. Even the few times that we've had some tax relief, we have later discovered that the gross tax burden has increased.

An analysis of the true burden of taxes has never exhibited anything but momentary relief in an ever-increasing trend. In current history, we saw a Reagan era tax cut that stimulated the economy over a fourteen-year span. Unfortunately, each successive tax bill eroded these benefits and imposed greater tax burdens. They were often responsible for the economic downturns during those years.

The 1997 Taxpayer Relief Act was a return to a Reagan-like tax stimuli formula. While this too will cause an economic boost to the national economy, history tells us that these momentary relief periods are followed by a siege of adverse tax bills that will sink us deeper in the bondage of taxation. The answer is not just taxpayer relief, it is government spending restraint. The latter is yet to be seen and frankly not in the cards.

The "Invisible Tax" is called **Inflation**. A 4% inflation rate over just seven years has the same impact as a 28% tax bite. That means your investment of $10,000 over a seven-year period will have the spending power of $7,200 at the end of the cycle.

In another example, let's suppose that you put your money in a bank account at 4% for ten years and we experience an average of 6% inflation over those same ten years. In this case, you will once again have the similar impact of a 28% erosion factor on your investment, which leaves $7,200 in spending power from the original $10,000 investment.

Some have referred to inflation as the "Boiled Frog Syndrome" where a frog is placed in tepid water, and a very miniscule flame raises the temperature gradually over time. Since the frog cannot detect small changes in temperature, he will stay in the water until he dies. Inflation is well described by this example.

You must invest your money effectively if you will stay ahead of either the overt tax affect of the government or the subtle tax affect of inflation. Therefore, an accumulation plan is necessary for a good estate plan, but you cannot reverse this statement since an accumulation plan is only part of estate planning.

There is yet another reason that your wealth will dissipate after you're gone. It is called **Dilution**! By this I mean that your wealth will be spread across your children (say three kids), and it will be spread out once again through your grandchildren (say nine grandchildren). This has a dilution factor of nine times. Therefore a half-million-dollar estate has the value of $90,000 to the grandchildren. Remember also that the detraction of taxation and inflation may make that $90,000 feel like $25,000. Not bad, but a far cry from what most families intend for their loved ones.

The final reason that your wealth will dwindle is **Devastation**. Unfortunately, you cannot reasonably expect that your family will not run into life-rattling problems. If not you, some ill wind will blow on your children and/or grandchildren. Problems such as: unemployment, illness, divorce, business failure, unexpected bills, children issues, IRS problems, and senior illnesses could easily strip your children of their personal wealth. Many of the things they will encounter can be resolved by better planning.

We suggest that the only way to counterbalance these adverse factors is a serious integration of "Wealth Leveraging" as a part of every true estate plan. The ability to leverage wealth is far more involved than compound interest. It is an artform combining the skills of investing, insurance, tax strategies, and estate planning concepts to conserve, protect and develop wealth through several generations. I find this particular skill sadly lacking among my peers whose concerns seem to be in "selling a product to the next prospect they meet."

We've all heard the Bible story told by Jesus of the man who built a tower and forgot to contemplate and forecast the final cost to finish. Having built several homes, I was surprised to learn that the investment of time and money to erect the shell of a building was often quicker and less expensive than all the work that went into the interior completion. As a result of this person's lack of vision, the tower went undone, and the people of the community referred to the tower as a folly instead of an accomplishment. And the good intentions of the builder now only speak to his lack of understanding.

In a similar way, I find most people mistake ample money for their needs as a bounty to their heirs. I have found that the surviving spouse will likely encounter more expenses than contemplated, and the majority of estates under three million do not significantly impact the generation of their grandchildren.

I occasionally hear the statement; "I have all the money I need and enough for my children." I am sure they are proud of their achievements, and I assume they are right because they have all the money they need.

I want to raise a thought that you need to consider, and that is the purpose of your measure of wealth. Do you believe you were given this portion of wealth so that you and your family will be insulated from potential problems, or might there be a greater purpose? I reject the thought that there is EVER enough money, because I see a world of homeless people, starving children, uncured diseases, scarce educational endowments, church needs, hospital pleas, and a thousand other desperate cries for money. The government is not the supplier of those needs. You are!

It is critical that the shortsighted and self-involved person realize that the world does not drop away three feet from where they live. If they look beyond their need and that of their family, they will get a vision of the real purpose of money. Do something worthy with it. Money is not just wealth, its a duty!

The duty of money is to serve man, not for man to serve money. Social capital is a matter we will discuss further, but it carries the implication and obvious necessity to make sure your money goes to programs that you believe in. The government is seldom anyone's idea of being socially responsible. Yet both the state of your residency and the federal government have made major efforts to collect large portions of your money to be spent in programs that would cause you to roll over in your grave.

IRS publishes a compendium of approved 501(c)(3) organizations. This list covers religious and non-religious programs. It covers every type of religion where you will discover a vast number of needs and programs that will be benefited by your gifts in life or death. I suggest that you explore the possibilities of what your money could do if you were to look beyond your family and realize that your endowment of wealth has a higher calling.

In this case, you will find working with a Certified Estate Plannerä will be a wonderful experience, and you will discover the taxable benefits you enjoy by planned giving of your estate that will also benefit your family and your world.

One of the secrets of the wealthy is that they get as much as a 500% return on every single dollar they give to charity. The tax breaks are huge, and even those with moderate incomes can still enjoy the same benefits by helping others who are not as fortunate.

Chapter 5
Illness and Medicaid

"We do not all pass quietly in the night"

It is not a pleasant thought that we will not enjoy good health in later life. In fact, 40% of Americans will require nursing home care, and 70% of married couples will have at least one spouse requiring nursing home care. We are told that one million Americans go broke every year due to the cost of senior illnesses and subsequently must apply for assistance from Medicaid.

Nursing home costs have currently grown from $35,000 to $45,000 per year, and the cost of "round the clock" care for a senior in their home adds up to about $100,000 per year. Statistically, 41% of such care is paid by the family, 51% is paid by Medicaid, 2% is paid by long term care insurance, veteran's benefits pay a small portion, and miscellaneous pays the rest. We are told that hospital care and nursing home care is growing faster than inflation. This means, you must anticipate some extraordinary costs for those still in their working years! We therefore see another reason why accumulation plans will not be sufficient for the total planning needs of the majority of Americans.

The recent introduction of the Kennedy-Kassebaum Act has added a new dimension to the rules for those requiring Medicaid assistance for nursing home costs.[13] If you attempt the typical "Asset

---

[13] HR3303 (also called HIPAA) was passed in 1996 and became law on 1/1/97. This sweeping law made Medicare and Medicaid the Federal Health Care system, and imposed many new restrictions for these agencies and those persons who use them.

Shift" to your children or other favored person in order to more quickly qualify for Medical assistance, you will now violate a federal criminal law. Violators will be subject to a $10,000 to $25,000 fine and one to five years in jail![14]

And yet, we all know what is going to happen, don't we? Every parent is going to try to conserve their wealth and protect their home. Fortunately, the Kennedy-Kassebaum Act was unenforceable and was eventually gutted of the criminal penalties. It remains to be seen what the government will do next to stop the hemorrhaging of money from the Medicaid system.

Of course, there are still other things that Medicaid can enforce. They have the ability to drive you into Forced Poverty by the Medicaid Spend Down, and they also have the abiltiy to capture the family home by imposing a lien on the home of the Medicaid recipient.

If Medicaid is an issue, there are just a few answers left. Long Term Care insurance is highly recommended for all seniors today. I, personally, recommend LTC policies. This removes the government from the issue and places it in the free enterprise system. With certain inconsistencies, the free market is capable of solving most problems we face. While there is a cost to private industry solutions, their fees are typically less onerous than more taxes! Let the insurance company pay the real cost while you pay only the premiums. Those that are incapable of paying should be shared in pools by the insurance industry as we do other uninsurable risks.

The second method is to divest away from your assets well in advance (36-60 months) before any occasion of nursing home need.[15]

---

[14] The good news is that the courts are expressing that this law is unenforceable and only the most blatant attempts of fraud will ever see any recourse but it will not be jail time. More likely civil sanctions will be applied to those who illegally hide assets.

[15] Any transfers from your estate must be done well in advance. Gifts from the client to another must be accomplished 36 months prior to Medicaid application. Gifts to trust must be accomplished 60 months prior to Medicaid application to avoid allegations of fraud.

The strategic use of annuities has also offered limited protection for many estates. Annuities are only a partial and desperate cure because you will lose a substantial part of the estate if you do need nursing home care and Medicaid assistance. A deferred annuity can be annuitized prior to application to Medicaid. While Medicaid could obtain the annuity payments during the person's life, the remaining payments go to the heirs at death. This gives some fairness to all parties.

The manner of divesting is almost always some form of irrevocable trust.[16] This moves ownership out of the senior's name but not into the name of the children yet. The premature gifting of assets to the children is a plan, but not a very good one! The other side of the issue is leaving enough income to the senior to make them secure.

Frankly, no one really wants to be under the care of Medicaid, but should rather reserve enough money to pay for his or her own care. In truth, Medicaid is hemorrhaging money and seems out of control. Congress tried to fix the problem by imposing the Kennedy-Kassebaum Act in 1996, but that law is a failure. I firmly believe Congress will never solve this problem. And their only answers will be taxation of everyone and restrictions on those who need serious help in their later years.

The goal of a planner is to protect your assets from abuse. He should also develop a strategy to help you without abusing this government program. The planner should not be desirous to cheat the government regardless of what you may think of it. Each side of this issue deserves consideration and neither should be abused or over emphasized. Fraud and evasion are never good tactics, and a good

---

[16] Be aware that irrevocable trusts mean you give your assets away to the protection of trustees. As a word of warning, NEVER allow a bank to be installed as trustee. When done through a bank, they entrench themselves so well that the senior and their heirs are devastated and there is no recourse.

plan can mediate a reasonable solution for all.

Another issue that remains until today was imposed in 1993 by OBRA. This tax act required in Title 42 that every state impose something called "Recovery Rules." These recovery rules demand that each state place liens on the real property of all Medicaid recipients. These liens are an attempt to recover money for Medicaid. This means that when the client dies, the probate court will transfer the assets of the deceased and pay off all creditors before paying anything to the heirs. In that Medicaid is a creditor with a legal claim against you through the lien, the probate court will turn your home over to Medicaid for settlement of your Medicaid bill.

Therefore, we face a two-fold financial bite. Medicaid forces a person to "Spend Down" all their assets to pay for their personal nursing home care until they are broke, but you can keep the home. Secondly, the Medicaid lien is used to strip away the remaining asset, the family home. The result is that the senior will be completely stripped of assets. Seniors have reason to be fearful of such policies, and children have reason to encourage Mom and Dad to take good steps in their planning. You'll never know the value of such planning until you encounter these crushing problems!

Chapter 6
The Illiquidity Trap
"When you're rich on paper, but poor at the bank"

Here's an example of the next problem we will discuss. You bought stocks or bonds over the years and held them through the 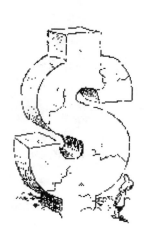 years. Today you may have more money in stocks and bonds than you ever thought you would amass. This sounds like a great problem to have until you decide to cash out of the investments. Guess what most people encounter that prevents them from selling their investments? A capital gain tax on most long-term gains of 10-20%, meaning a $200,000 gain will produce a $40,000 tax.[17] Not a fun idea, huh?

Or consider a person, perhaps a farmer, who bought land many years ago and now it is worth far more than the meager purchase price. They once again encounter a similar capital gain tax if they sell the property with the intention of enjoying the profits.

Frankly, I have had people who said, "I will die before I sell that asset and pay those kind of taxes." And you know what? That is exactly what happened.

---

[17] Capital Gain Tax is a tax imposed on any sale where there is a profit realized at sale. This tax is paid with your normal income tax each year unless you defer the taxable event. Deferral is not a simple task, but achievable.

This is what we mean by being illiquid. You may have sizable assets but you can't get at the cash without incurring taxes, fees, delays, and market demands. We call it rich on paper (net worth statement), but poor at the bank (cash). Taxes are often the culprit that creates illiquidity. Federal Estate Tax forces an estate to pay the full 37-55% tax exactly nine months after a death. Such cash demands are an incredible pressure on the heirs and force estate sales under distressed conditions. Perhaps you've seen estate sales advertised in your local newspapers. These sales are an effort to liquidate the assets in order to pay the probate costs and/or taxes due on the estate. The estate is further punished because such distressed sales rarely bring an honest price.

Capital gains tax is the other tax that forces us to part with cash to Uncle Sam. With the run up of the stock market and land prices, a vast number of seniors have this problem, and they have no idea what to do to alleviate the tax bite. They are trapped. At this time, they ought to be able to sell off those investments and make the best of their senior years. Instead, they sit at home watching Oprah and listening to their arteries harden.

In fact, there are only three ways to deal with capital gain tax or most any tax:

1) **Pay the tax** as it comes due
2) **Defer the Taxable Event** through proper planning
3) **Eliminate the Tax** by step-up at death or charitable gift

Admittedly, number one is not the most inviting ... but it is safe! I recommend that you choose a plan that you not only like, but that you are willing to accomplish. Most people like number two and three, but are not willing to do the work necessary to achieve either one. So, if you're super conservative, just pay the tax and free up the money. Seniors seldom like aggressive tax tactics. Wealth on paper is not very helpful to most people. Regardless of your choice, do not simply allow such issues to be ignored. Illiquidity can be resolved, but ignorance is not the answer!

Deferral is achieved when we are able to cash out the investment but delay the full receipt of the money until some future date. There are four ways to achieve deferral in such matters:

1) Installment sale of assets
2) Private Annuities that pay you over time
3) Like kind exchanges under IRC 1031-1035
4) Certain irrevocable trusts that move assets by exchange under IRC 1015 related to 453(g) and 721(a)

If you sell an appreciated asset to someone on an installment plan, you are perfectly legitimate in deferring the taxable event through approved IRS methods. Installment payments are a perfect example of selling an asset and deferring the taxable event. Deferral is popular because you generally have a measure of control or management over the asset. Then 100% of the sale price can be invested and may grow to produce a larger future return. As the word deferral infers, these tactics only delay the tax for a future event when you'll pay the tax as you withdraw. Deferral is not elimination of taxes, deferral delays the taxable event.

If you want to eliminate the tax, you must either give the assets to charity or die using a program that steps-up the basis.[18] A direct gift to charity means you only get the tax deduction for the gift, but that isn't bad. In fact, charitable gifting allows you to fulfill a measure of social and ethical obligation regarding the purpose of your portion of wealth. In a simple analysis, the wealth you have been

---

[18] Step-Up at Death: IRC 1014 states that an asset held by the decedent in such a device as a living trust will have a step-up in the basis to equal the fair market value. This means there will be no applicable capital gain tax after the death of the trustor who funded the trust.

given should not be dissipated by taxes and fees because of the intrusion of government and attorneys. The duty of money is to use it well and meaningfully. Direct charitable gifts and charitable trusts are ways to make sure your money goes for more effective and overall good in this world in which you live. The virtue of delaying the gift to charity by a trust is that you can enjoy the interest yield during your lifetime providing you with the finest retirement plan you'll ever find.

If you use a charitable remainder trust, the gift is not made immediately to the charity, but is held to produce an income for the grantor (you) for your life. Additionally, you get a tax deduction in the year you make the contribution to the charitable trust which makes the idea very inviting. If the asset contributed has capital gain that would be taxable, it will be eliminated in the charitable trust. The numerous virtues of a charitable remainder trust must be explored with an open mind, but you'll find it very worth the effort to pursue.

A Private Annuity is set up by a skilled attorney and allows you to dispose of an appreciated asset to another buyer. The buyer promises to pay you an annuitized payment for the rest of your life. The impact of any gain is deferred but the payment you receive is partially taxable and partially basis (non-taxed). This is best accomplished by using an offshore entity to purchase and sell the asset for you to avoid family and government constraints. Generally, private annuities are reserved for large assets since the cost to accomplish this task is larger than a charitable trust. If you want to dispose of a business, large stock portfolio, or real estate; the private annuity is a great and effective device.

If you want to eliminate the tax, you must either give the assets to charity or die.[19] I prefer the first choice because we can still get a lifetime of beneficial enjoyment out of the payments that come to us

---

[19] Step-Up at Death refers to a section of IRC 1014(b) where the code allows us to replace the basis with the current fair market value at the day of death and completely eliminate the occurrence of capital gain.

from the Charitable Trust. The gift to trust of an appreciated asset is simple, but you can retain the right to income from the trust for your lifetime and that of your spouse. The wealth only goes to the charity at the second death. Your children are amply rewarded by a special policy that replaces the gifted wealth and pays benefits tax-free. When examined closely, you will find that the Charitable Trust is likely the best of all solutions. However, it does take a properly trained person to explain, structure, and implement this kind of plan.

Finally, you should know that all capital gain is washed out at death as assets are transferred by Will and/or Trusts. This is a great tax relief, and it is rare to find benevolence in the tax code (IRC 1014). The obvious problem is that you only get this benefit when you die, and most people would like to free up their money prior to death and enjoy it to some measure.

Paying taxes is a simple fact of life. I am not recommending that you employ any of these features unless you are comfortable with the concepts. Too many people want to have their cake and eat it too.

There is a challenge to estate and tax planning. You do not simply get these benefits because you like the idea. You must adopt the idea and take methodic steps to accomplish your goal. Deferral of tax is not automatic but an intentional action. Elimination of tax may require that you divest of ownership to get the desired effect. Please be aware that tax planning comes at a cost, but the good news is that it often returns far, far more in return. Regardless of your charitable or benevolent reservations, tax planning may give you benefits that are worth the effort.

Notation: The IRS has stipulated that any plan or device that is established for the singular purpose of tax avoidance (avoidance is legal, evasion is illegal) will be considered a sham. The answer is rather simple however. Your motive for your estate plan could be estate preservation to your loved ones, a business continuation plan, an investment consideration, avoidance of probate, and wealth development. There are many other reasons to complete an estate plan and therefore your intent is not purely avoidance of taxation. Do not be dissuaded by this argument (tax avoidance as a sham) since it lacks any sense of real world experience.

Chapter 7
Three Levels of Estate Planning

"Consumers are sheep, good only for shearing"

Let's move to the underlying premise of estate planning and consider from a more neutral viewpoint how to plan your affairs. The first issue is crucial to getting your life and affairs under control. You should not do business with people who are singular in their abilities. By this I mean something very important is being neglected because of their limitations. When working with advisors who have impressed us with their abilities on one level, we foolishly credit them with total trust to handle all issues of life.

I have said that attorneys are not estate planners. The same is true of accountants, insurance people, security and investment people, and so on. There is a need for professional estate planners who will do more than sell a product under the guise of estate planning. These Certified Estate Plannersä are uniquely capable of bringing together the virtues of various aspects of the services you need to develop a true estate plan which addresses all your needs instead of the piece-meal effect that you have now.

Be wary of secret alliances between attorneys, accountants, insurance people, and investment advisors to pass the client around to the next guy in line. And the amazing thing is that the client obediently allows himself to be shuttled back and forth thinking that these people will take care of them. On the contrary, I would want one knowledgeable person to draw out a map or proposal that outlined all my needs and address specific solutions. I do not want to go blindly from one professional office to the next having the money artfully extracted from my wallet by various advisors.

The second scene is equally bad. Instead of being referred around by these guys, I decide to go from office to office and figure my estate planning needs out independently. This is commendable but an exercise in frustration. In essence, you will experience the distress of having advisor after advisor attempt to pull you to their particular program. Estate planning combines the virtues of many professional strategies into one cohesive plan designed just for you.

The coach is neither the lineman nor the backfield. He directs the players. He needs to employ the skills of various players on the team to win the game. He may not play all the positions, but he may be essential to a winning season. A coach must know all the positions and his influence is seen in each player and position for proper execution.

An orchestra needs a conductor to create the beautiful music that we enjoy. Separately, each player and instrument may do a fine job of playing, but cannot match the majesty and power of a well-directed orchestra. Regardless of the advisor you use, unless he/she is fully developed in estate planning, he/she is inadequate to complete the necessary estate plan for your life.

An Estate Planner, like a coach and conductor, must be able to function on three levels of expertise and incorporate numerous tactics. Nearly every one of the self-anointed estate planners, knows only the first of these three levels. Nonetheless, it is vital that the plan includes, in some measure, all three aspects:

1) **Estate Preservation**: The ability to pass your estate with little or no erosion to your heirs.
2) **Asset Protection**: The ability to protect your estate from civil issues during your lifetime.
3) **Leveraging of Wealth**: The ability to structure your wealth over several generations.

Generally, such planning as wills or revocable living trusts are simply estate preservation and devoid of the other two elements. Your children will be pleased that you have provided for their future, but you may suffer from other forms of trouble in the general estate plan.

When you think about estate planning, most people tend to think that all attorneys do estate planning. This is wrong! Some attorneys do estate planning, most just take a stab at it. Not all doctors practice heart or brain surgery, but that doesn't mean any doctor can't try such an operation. They are licensed, and with a little brushing up most doctors could do a semblance of those medical specialties. And almost any attorney can buy the books or software to do estate planning, but that is a far cry from someone who really knows estate planning.

Estate planning requires several skills that may not be found in most professionals. The preparation of documents requires an attorney, but the other issues of retirement planning, tax planning, investing needs, and advanced concepts are often neglected in the belief that a document is all that is needed.

There are three primary areas of true estate planning

Estate Preservation: The ability to pass your estate to the next generation with minimal delay and erosion. This is commonly done through Revocable Living Trusts and associated documents.

What the planner attempts to accomplish is to avoid the factors called "erosion." This means the accumulated losses from probate, federal estate tax, excise tax, capital gain tax, and court appointed guardianship. If we avoid these erosions, we will have effectively preserved the estate for the heirs. Estate preservation is a notable and important task that is worthy of the effort.

Asset Protection is the ability to protect your assets during your lifetime so that no civil action or potential creditor can relieve you of your wealth. Unless you can protect the assets in your lifetime there may not be anything to preserve.

Lawsuits, divorce, bankruptcy, creditor claims, IRS demands, Medicaid, and financial failures are some of the possibilities that warrant protection of our assets.

Leveraged Wealth: The ability to structure your assets in the provided legal format so as to maximize the wealth to you, your children, and your grandchildren beyond simple investing ideas. Leveraged wealth is the ability to strategically create multi-generational wealth.

The American family has serious issues demanding that you consider more than an investment or accumulation plan. Three negative factors will cause your wealth to evaporate much more rapidly than you might expect:

A) Taxation: The cumulative impact of layers of taxation on your income, estate, appreciation, and transfer of wealth can strip away 30-70% of your estate.

B) Inflation: The hidden tax that may reduce your estate by 28% per decade, making your gains seem minor.

C) Dilution: If you have three children, and then nine grand children, you must divide the resultant estate by nine and mi nus out the spending of the three children to calculate what might be left to your grandchildren.

D) Devastation: No family is exempted from tragedy, and the likelihood that you or your children or grandchildren may incur some form of devastation could eliminate even sizable wealth in that generation.

The emphasis is that we must consider well-developed concepts in the planning process to assure that our money makes it to more than one generation. In 1996 during the battle between President Clinton and Newt Gingrich over the budget, Clinton explained that if we didn't get our budget balanced, our children would pay a tax rate of 84%. Sounds incredible, but certainly tells us where things are headed. In light of these factors, you cannot say that you have enough money. Such limited insight will guarantee that the people you love dearly will not have the headstart in life you want them to have.

Preserve your estate, protect your assets, and do not mildly believe that your modest financial plan is sufficient in itself. We emphatically insist that every estate plan must integrate the three factors of estate planning, or suffer from the potential of unforeseen and unplanned disasters.

Epilogue
Three Rules of True Wealth

"A rut is only a grave with the ends kicked out"

There are "Ten Commandments of Money and Wealth" which form my philosophy about money. I find it odd that we work for money all our adult lives, handle it every single day, and build our lives around the acquisition of it for our retirement. But, to be very honest, we really do not know what it is or how it truly works. And yet, throughout my life I have discovered that there are certain actions and attitudes that can be used to develop wealth, which I call the Ten Commandments of Money and Wealth. This will greatly benefit those who want to know the principles of financial success.

There are ten commandments, but I will not have the opportunity to share them all in this material. However, I would like to give you the first three that form the thesis for all the rest. Much like the original Ten Comandments, the first three directives hold the keys to the remaining seven. It will take you some time to understand what I am about to say, but you will be surprised that you will recognize what I am saying as true. Such is the nature of truisms. We all seem to acknowledge that something is true even though we may not practice it. Every time I hear someone say that I should change the oil in my car every three thousand miles, I know they're right, but I don't do it because it is not convenient. I also know the car will not wear as well if I don't, but I justify it by saying that I won't keep it long enough to find out. I don't debate the truth about oil changes, but I still find myself not doing what I should in the matter.

In some ways it would be like playing a game that you did not understand. We try to draw from experiences that do not correlate to this new game. We all think we ought to know how to succeed in life and protect ourselves from problems. We're not children, disabled, nor without normal intellectual skills; and yet we do not understand these fundamentals. Other than sheer luck and unmerited inheritances, the rest of us find that money is a constant mystery that we never really figure out. The few that do, we envy and would like to know why they are so fortunate. But money has rules just like any fact of life. Sir Isaac Newton DID NOT discover gravity, but he did figure it out. He experimented until he knew the laws of gravity. How long did it take to figure out the world was round? Those sailors who ventured beyond charted waters were afraid of falling off the edge. Finally, why did Europe have to endure the Black Plague until they finally learned the basics of sanitation, germs, and contagion? None of these items were new, but the understanding of them took the world a long time to figure out.

So, let's look at the number one statement. We must define the object of our study. In the law, we are told that if the premise is flawed, then all that follows is flawed as well. Much of the financial distress of this world starts with a misunderstanding of what money is. When improperly understood, *MONEY ENGENDERS GREED*. Therefore, you can see that we're already in a lot of trouble when it comes to money. And, even if you suffer from the most mild case of greed, you will find that *GREED POLLUTES HAPPINESS*. I am not afraid of money as long as I understand it. It is not riches that lead to evil, we are told. It is the *Love of Money (Greed)* that causes so much of our financial distress.

I hope you are careful to pay attention here. As with every premise, the impact of the succeeding statements can only be understood when the premise is clear. Therefore, as a primer on money, let's discuss exactly what money is. The result will be success, happiness, and security.

MONEY IS A RESOURCE

Every single time you hear any thing about money, you will hear it spoken of in quantitative terms. Money is always discussed in how much or how little of it that you possess. Every point of reference we make about money is built upon some measurement. We have "net worth statements," "balance sheets," and "portfolio statements." We measure the success of our business by "cash flow statements," "profit and loss statements," and "accounts recievable and payable."

However, this concept is fundamentally flawed by the belief that money can only be defined by measurement. This flaw leads to some infection of a non-virtue called GREED. Money was not meant to be anything more than a medium, not an animate object that seems to have a life of its own.[20] Instead of being in control, greed animates money to exert control over us.

We've been told that money is an unruly servant and a hard taskmaster. Money can rule us only as long as we are ignorant of the truth and follow its misguided logic. Once we learn its secret, we have the ability to master it for the first time in our lives.

Let's examine my premise to see if the thesis is obvious. Do you know any rich people that are unhappy, divorced, lives messed up, and generally harmed by wealth? I can imagine that you are smiling your answer. And do you know any poor people who seem to get

---

[20] A medium is not an object. A painter may work in the mediums of oils, watercolor, chalk, or marble, but none of these by themselfves are the art work. The artist uses the medium of choice to create the works of art that we appreciate. I don't like all art because it seems that some artists have lost touch with reality, but other art makes sense and may be enjoyed. Neither do I appreciate what other people do with their money, nor how they teach others that "more is better" because more is not the solution to any of the real issues of life.

ther very most out of life, their marriage, and have wonderful children? The answer is obvious. Neither group is universally happy or without trials and tribulation. All I am trying to say is that the AMOUNT of wealth has very little to do with happiness, marital success, or good kids.

Here's just one more example. Is there any real number that you can offer that can be achieved in the pursuit of money? When J. Paul Getty was asked *how much money is enough*, he replied, "Just one dollar more than I have right now!" If wealth is your pursuit, there will be moments when you see a beautiful house, car, or boat that will not make you feel any better about your situation. If you have one million dollars, you will want two million. If you have two million, you will want five million. And if you have five million, you will want ten million. So, what I am saying is that when you measure money there is no standard except your greed, ability, and life expectancy. When there is no standard, there is no truth!

OWNERSHIP IS A MYTH

Do you realize that you really can't own anything? At best, you are just renting time and space, and eventually you'll be gone. The whole myth of ownership has a fatal flaw. If you think you own a piece of property, stop paying your land tax for two years and see how the government will sell the property out from under you. Or stop paying your mortgage for six months and watch the bank repossess the property. Perhaps you might lose a serious lawsuit and realize that someone else can take your property from you regardless of your innocence.

Ownership should really be replaced with trusteeship or stewardship. You have only the temporary ability to manage assets under your control. Either death or adverse circumstances will eventually separate the most fierce grip from all the possessions of life. IRS has successfully stripped assets from people for generations. Civil courts currently shift assets from millions of families every year to their legal opponents. We are all aware that it is possible to lose everything, but most would rather enjoy the present benefits of ownership no matter how vulnerable their assets may be.

Ownership is a "legal right" recognized by the state as something you are allowed. Since we retain this right of ownership, guess who can obtain this legal right? The answer is anyone who can get the court's sanction can get to your assets.

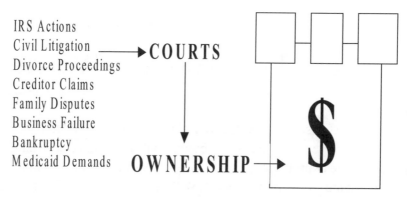

IRS Actions
Civil Litigation ———▶ **COURTS**
Divorce Proceedings
Creditor Claims
Family Disputes
Business Failure
Bankruptcy
Medicaid Demands **OWNERSHIP** ——▶ **$**

Your ownership is a legal right that can provide the bridge to your assets. If the court awards the legal right (because of your ownership) to anyone with a legal claim, you lose!

Since ownership is the legal right to your assets, anyone who can obtain the court's permission can reach your assets. Invasion of your assets is exactly what you want to avoid. But in order to forbid others the legal right to your assets, you must assume the same position as that of your creditor possession ... you must be a non-owner! Once you remove the bridge to your assets, other creditors cannot cross over and obtain those assets.

Trusts are once again the best means of transferring ownership because you can retain certain contractual or beneficial rights to the assets. Such contractual or beneficial rights are very hard for courts to reach or attach. Corporations, partnerships, and trusts alter the manner of ownership from personal ownership. Of these choices, trusts are perhaps the most effective.

These two critical facts form the foundation of another book from The Liberty Institute called the *Ten Commandments of Money and Wealth*. This book was written to correct many of the common, but improper facts about money. It may be purchased at The Liberty Institute bookstore. (http://www.libertyinstitute.com/books.html).

WRONG PERCEPTIONS OF WEALTH

As I summarize the *Ten Commandments of Money and Wealth* for people, it becomes obvious that people have been taught to operate contrary to the truth. They desire to own everything in their name (or in joint ownership), they have no solid plan for the distribution of their wealth, they borrow as much as they can possibly afford, and they do not accumulate money correctly.

We were all raised in similar fashion and the better character-istics were generally eroded away by financial and peer pressure over time. Our desire to own and enjoy various property and necessities serves to feed the burning desire to borrow money for what we deem to be important to us.

The fact that we BORROW money defeats our ability to save and accumulate wealth. The desire to OWN all of our assets in our own names or in joint tenancy traps us. We allow ourselves to be involuntarily divested by TAXATION and LITIGATION. We allow ourselves to be led about by advisors that are not well accomplished in estate planning. We ignore the SOCIAL ETHICS of applying our wealth according to our belief system. From our early years, we fall into cycles of behavior that work against the faithful constants of wealth and estate planning.

There are rules for gravity and every other economic program, and yet most people are grossly ingnorant of the operation and rules of money. Frankly, it is a near necessity that people go back to school to learn the things they didn't learn the first time. Who knew life was so complex and punishing? I have found that the older that I get, the more I realize that I just "didn't have a clue." I've also learned that I need to become smarter to avoid the mistakes of my past.

Habits are easily formed
But difficult to break
And possibly, too dearly embraced

Breaking the cycle of these habits means we must identify them and finally come to grips with changing them. The purpose of this book is to introduce you to the financial realities of life and your wealth. For those who've taken the time to come with me for a journey through stark problems and creative solutions, you have time to change your future through adapting these principles.

Ultimately, you must formulate your own financial and estate plan or rely on the mercy and wisdom of the court system. The probate court system is a default program that does what you did not do. It will resolve your estate issues in its own discretion with delays and costs that should not be required. Do not leave to others (and strangers) the job that you should do yourself.

Regardless of what products you've previously purchased, counselor you may have trusted, or lawyer that boasts his talent, you need a brand new look at your life and future. None of us are experts on these subjects, and we do need the help of reliable people who have more to gain than our money. Our experience with product providers and accumulation-type planners should show us that there is a need for something better and more effective in design and care of our life's assets.

Neither insurance or investments are estate plans! The amount in your bank account does not stave off a lawsuit. Neither does the quality of your character protect you from the adversities of life. We are all subject to the common ailments of life. The smart ones plan for adversity before it visits their door. The rest simply endure, hope, and sometimes fail ... all for a lack of planning!

Sit down today with a Certified Estate Planner and have this professional design a plan that resolves your issues. Consider these new paradigms that have been offered and be prepared for solutions that can make a difference.

For good or bad, dear friend...
This is Your Life

Conclusion
Why America Chooses Trusts
"The Self-Defense of the American Public"

There is another phenomenon in America today that is frankly anti-establishment or at least counter-culture. The groundswell popularity of trusts has made the legal and financial world sit back and take note. This movement is what I call a "Bottom-Up" instead of "Top-Down" where the public is demanding and seeking out better plans than those being offered by the schooled advisors.

Like many professions, the practice of law and the accounting services are somewhat incestuous in that they germinate all information from within their own breeding pool. The Ivy League schools have taught them all in the same didactic manner and turned out a legal and accounting clone who does not deviate from the accepted dogma of their peers. In fact, a CPA will generally stand to attention and salute if you say the word GAAP which stands for "Generally Accepted Accounting Procedures." GAAP means an accountant will not do anything that has not been done ten thousand times before and was supported by tax court. An attorney and a CPA must obtain CPE (Continuing Professional Education) each year to keep their licenses current, and they typically hear and learn what they've already been taught.

While we may commend their educational accomplishments and professional credential pursuit, we have found that the minor variations in these professions are very prejudicial and antithetic to any ideas that did not start with them. In fact, some have suggested that these industries suffer from the NIH syndrome (Not Invented Here). Hence, there is a knee-jerk and predictable hesitation toward anything not accepted among their peers.

The first entry of the trust industry was the Revocable Living Trust. In the early years (1980s), we saw a slow and persistent growth in popularity, effectiveness, and demand for the Revocable Living Trust. In those same years, attorneys and accountants did everything but call them voodoo. Accountants claimed they had to file a separate tax report (they didn't during the grantor's lifetime). Attorneys said they were too expensive and too laborious, and then encouraged their clients to stick with wills and endure the cost and delays of probate. The irony seems to be lost on all but those who saw it firsthand.

The rise of the business and non-grantor trust was another "bottom-up revolution" decried by the "top-down establishment." Armed with a few cases where trusts had been abused, they denounced them all as "shams" hoping that this time they would suffer from an advanced form of crib death. Once again, they have failed and now these trusts have flourished in America as they had many years before. However, it still is your life, and you are capable of making your own decisions.

What is a Trust? The classic definition is a contractual arrangement whereby one person holds property for the benefit of another. The assets or property that you put into a trust are called "corpus" or "res." A trust without assets is really a defunct entity. Be very cautious of creating a trust without a serious plan to transfer or fund the trust.

What is a Grantor/Trustor? The person who creates and funds the trust is considered the grantor, trustor, or settlor. This person changes the ownership of the assets to the name of the trust to accomplish a more efficient transfer of wealth, mitigate tax and probate costs, and even provide some asset protection.

What is a Trustee? A trustee is also a fiduciary who has a duty to fulfill the demands of the trust. A trustee is not an owner, cannot act in his/her own self-interest, and administrates the trust until it is dispersed to the beneficiaries.

What is a Beneficiary? The ultimate owner of assets (currently unrealized) is the beneficiary. They may have no present rights (unless named as trustees), but will one day inherit the assets currently owned in the trust if not otherwise disposed of in the lifetime of the grantor.

The most common form of trust is a Revocable Living Trust which allows the grantor rights of revocation, invasion, and management although everything is in the trust. Other forms of trust are irrevocable and they are typically funded only with life insurance in an effort to inexpensively pay off federal estate tax or provide a tax-free inheritance to the children. Generally, the Revocable Living Trust can only protect a little over $625,000 for a single person or $1,250,000 for a married couple. If your estate is over that figure, you will use the Irrevocable Life Insurance Trust (called an ILIT) to hold a block of life insurance that will offset the anticipated federal estate tax bill. A planner should assist to make sure the insurance anticipates life expectancy and anticipated growth of the estate.

Jacqueline Kennedy Onassis

and her $200 million estate TAX FREE

PERSONALITY PARADE®

Q *I'm not clear about the fortune left by Jacqueline Kennedy Onassis when she died this year. Can you give us some details?—M.A. Baker, Canyon, Tex.*

A Press releases said Mrs. Onassis' 36-page will valued her estate at "greater than $500,000." That's a conservative figure. In fact, her net worth was at least $200 million when Jackie died at 64. The bulk of it went to her children, Caroline, 37, and John, 34: $250,000 each in cash, plus trust funds set up by President Kennedy and the former First Lady. The two also received Jackie's 15-room Fifth Avenue co-op, her 425-acre estate on Martha's Vineyard, jewelry, art, furniture and cars. Her sister, Lee, 61, received nothing, because Jackie had taken care of her while alive. But Lee's children—Tony, 34, and Anna, 33—each got a $500,000 trust fund. Jackie's stepbrother, Hugh Auchincloss Jr., received her property in Newport, R.I. Jackie also left $100,000 to her niece, Alexandra Rutherford, and $250,000 to her spokeswoman, Nancy Tuckerman. Her longtime companion, Maurice Tempelsman, 65, received an ancient Greek sculpture. As one of the executors of Jackie's estate, however, he also may collect a hefty fee. Various organizations also will receive donations through the C&J Foundation, a charitable trust.

> Jacqueline Kennedy Onassis
>
> $200 million estate valued at $500,000.

68

The Last Will and Testament of
CHIEF JUSTICE WARREN BURGER

BOOK 156 PAGE 96
#22774

LAST WILL AND TESTAMENT
OF
WARREN E. BURGER

I hereby make and declare the following to be my last will and testament.

1. My exeuctors will first pay all claims against my estate;

2. The remainder of my estate will be distributed as follows: one-third to my daughter, Margaret Elizabeth Burger Rose and two-thirds to my son, Wade A. Burger;

3. I designate and appoint as executors of this will, Wade A. Burger and J. Michael Luttig.

IN WITNESS WHEREOF, I have hereunto set my hand to this my Last Will and Testament this ___9th___ day of June, 1994.

Warren E. Burger
WARREN E. BURGER

We hereby certify that in our presence on the date written above WARREN E. BURGER signed the foregoing instrument and declared it to be his Last Will and Testament and that at this request in his presence and in the presence of each other we have signed our names below as witnesses.

_____ residing at 120 'F' St, NW
Washington, DC

_____ residing at 3041. Meetig. St
~~FAIRFAX VA~~ Falls Church, VA

SWORN TO AND SUBSCRIBED BEFORE ME THIS 9th

A Copy,
Teste: David A. Bell, Clerk   DAY OF June , 19 94

By _____
Deputy Clerk

Constance Y. Ferguson
NOTARY PUBLIC

CONSTANCE Y. FERGUSON
Notary Public, District of Columbia
My Commission Expires January 31, 1999

For more information on estate planning check us out on the Internet.

The Virtual University - General Education
http://www.tvu.org

The Liberty Institute - Books and Professional Education
http://www.libertyinstitute.com

Find a Certified Estate Planner in your area at
http://www.nccep.cc